Would You You Rather?

Pick **THIS** or **THAT**

Weird, Wacky, or Downright Gross Answer

PETER PAUPER PRESS, INC.
Rye Brook, New York

PETER PAUPER PRESS

In 1928, at the age of twenty-two, Peter Beilenson began printing books on a small press in the basement of his parents' home in Larchmont, New York. Peter—and later, his wife, Edna—sought to create fine books that sold at "prices even a pauper could afford."

Today, still family owned and operated, Peter Pauper Press continues to honor our founders' legacy of quality, value, and fun for big kids and small kids alike.

Designed by Heather Zschock
Images used under license from Shutterstock.com

Copyright © 2023
Peter Pauper Press, Inc.
3 International Drive
Rye Brook, NY 10573 USA

Published in the United Kingdom and Europe by
Peter Pauper Press, Inc. c/o White Pebble International
Units 2-3, Spring Business Park
Stanbridge Road
Havant, Hampshire PO9 2GJ, UK

Visit us at www.peterpauper.com

Any Questions?

Did you know that you make hundreds of choices every day? It's true! Whenever you decide how to wear your hair, or what to eat for breakfast, you are using logic and creativity to think things through. You may not realize it, but whenever you make these decisions, you're playing a real-life version of **Would You Rather**, sizing up the options in front of you and choosing what's best.

These daily choices might seem trivial, but sometimes just asking the question is where all the fun lies. With this book, you're given 280 hilarious and hard-hitting scenarios to exercise your decision-making skills, show off your creativity, and laugh out loud!

Use this book to start a conversation, or, if you're playing with friends, make a game out of it. Here are some tips to get started:

- With your group, choose one person to act as the judge, who will be responsible for reading a question aloud to the group.

- Players will then answer the question and explain their reasoning.

- The judge chooses the winning answer—this can be the answer that's funniest, most creative, or best defended!

- Winner judges the next question!

There's no one out there who thinks exactly like you, and that's a good thing! So, would you rather get a group together and play a round, or turn the page now and start imagining the possibilities yourself?

No Question . . . 5
Head Scratchers . . . 40
Weighing the Scales . . . 75
Impossible to Answer . . . 110

No Question

Would you rather have one best friend

OR

five friends who you're not that close with?

Would you rather get caught farting loudly

OR

picking your nose?

**Would you rather
be stuck on a
deserted island**

OR

in a mysterious forest?

**Would you rather be
able to control when
it rains**

OR

when it snows?

Would you rather have the power of invisibility

OR

the power of flight?

Would you rather sing everything you say

OR

dance anytime you walk?

Would you rather have eyes that film whatever you see

OR

ears that record whatever you hear?

Would you rather have to eat everything with a fork

OR

have to eat everything with a spoon?

Would you rather
wear a shirt one size
too small

OR

wear shoes two
sizes too big?

Would you rather have toes for fingers

OR

fingers for toes?

Would you rather be three feet shorter

OR

five feet taller than you currently are?

Would you rather have chameleon skin

OR

a monkey tail?

Would you rather always be underdressed

OR

overdressed for events?

Would you rather be a wizard

OR

a superhero?

Would you rather be the strongest person alive

OR

the fastest?

Would you rather be the hero in a science fiction universe

OR

in a magical fantasy land?

Would you rather be a centaur

OR

a mermaid?

Would you rather travel everywhere by unicycle

OR

tricycle?

Would you rather
have to walk everywhere
on stilts

OR

have to go barefoot?

Would you rather be
a famous actor

OR

a famous musician?

Would you rather have
webbed feet

OR

webbed hands?

Would you rather have unlimited pizza

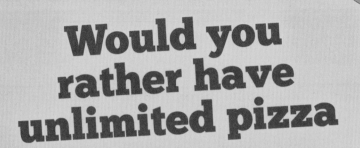

OR

tacos for life?

Would you rather read a book a week

OR

never read a book again?

Would you rather only be able to watch movies in your house

OR

in a movie theater?

Would you rather go
to sleep every night in
a hammock

OR

a sleeping bag?

Would you rather all
water tastes like your
favorite drink

OR

all vegetables taste
like your favorite
dessert?

17

Would you rather perform with your favorite singer

OR

play sports with your favorite athlete?

Would you rather have to walk to school every day through knee-deep mud

OR

knee-deep snow?

Would you rather take a deep sniff from someone's armpit

OR

from someone's feet?

Would you rather design a skyscraper

OR

design the next big video game?

Would you rather build a base on the moon

OR

go to the deepest parts of the ocean in a submarine?

Would you rather sleep over at the zoo

OR

sleep over at the aquarium?

**Would you rather
have a blobfish**

OR

**a naked mole rat
as a pet?**

**Would you rather travel
around the woods on
Bigfoot's back**

OR

**sail around on
the Loch Ness
Monster?**

Would you rather pull off a bank heist with your friends

OR

have your friends help you solve an ancient mystery?

Would you rather work as a lion tamer

OR

a rodeo clown?

Would you rather swim in a pool of maple syrup

OR

marshmallow fluff?

Would you rather have a personal assistant

OR

a personal chef?

Would you rather get trapped in the middle of a food fight

OR

in the middle of a water balloon fight?

Would you rather spend a snow day by the fireplace

OR

outside building a fort?

Would you rather have the superpower of your choice

OR

wake up every day with a new (random) superpower?

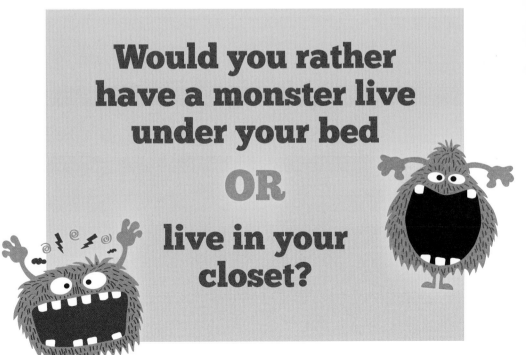

Would you rather have a monster live under your bed

OR

live in your closet?

Would you rather have a fart noise

OR

a burp as your ringtone?

Would you rather eat nothing but salad

OR

nothing but ice cream for a week?

Would you rather climb to the peak of a mountain

OR

explore a sunken ship?

Would you rather have a permanent puppy

OR

a permanent kitten?

Would you rather have a dog with a cat's personality

OR

a cat with a dog's personality?

Would you rather have a constantly itchy nose

OR

constantly itchy feet?

Would you rather have the world's biggest trampoline

OR

the world's tallest swing set?

Would you rather parachute out of an airplane

OR

bungee jump off a cliff?

Would you rather be a werewolf who spends one night of the month as a wolf and the rest as a human

OR

one who spends one night of the month as a human and the rest as a wolf?

Would you rather have
giant bird wings

OR

giant bat wings?

Would you rather make
a guest appearance on
your favorite TV show

OR

be invited to a big
movie premiere?

Would you rather be able
to slide down rainbows

OR

bounce on clouds?

Would you rather
only read books

OR

only watch movies?

Would you rather have
X-ray vision

OR

supersonic hearing?

Would you rather have to walk everywhere backwards

OR

hop everywhere on one foot?

Would you rather have a cat's ears

OR

retractable claws?

33

Would you rather be captured by pirates

OR

captured by an evil king's guards?

Would you rather have a dog the size of a hamster

OR

a hamster the size of a dog?

Would you rather have a bottomless plate of your favorite food

OR

a bottomless cup of your favorite drink?

Would you rather always have a pebble stuck in your shoe

OR

an itchy tag you can't remove from your shirt?

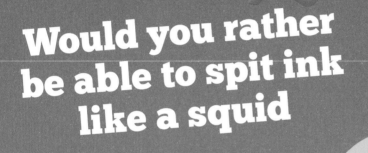

Would you rather be able to spit ink like a squid

OR

spray stinky liquid like a skunk?

Would you rather be the funniest person on Earth

OR

the smartest person on Earth?

Would you rather be late to every party

OR

arrive at every party too early?

Would you rather have a giraffe neck

OR

an elephant trunk?

Would you rather live in a mansion with your worst enemy

OR

a dumpster with your best friend?

Would you rather give up cheese in France

OR

fruit in the Bahamas?

**Would you rather
have a giant coral reef
aquarium at home**

OR

**a giant jungle-like
greenhouse at home?**

**Would you rather wear
a super-warm parka
on a hot summer day**

OR

**a T-shirt in a
snowstorm?**

Head Scratchers

Would you rather be able to speak with animals

OR

read people's minds?

Would you rather be the best in the world at one skill

OR

be pretty good at everything?

Would you rather be the best player on a team that always loses

OR

the worst player on a team that always wins?

Would you rather fight ten chicken-sized gorillas

OR

one gorilla-sized chicken?

Would you rather never brush your teeth again

OR

never brush your hair again?

Would you rather sneeze whenever you say hello

OR

get a case of the hiccups whenever you ask a question?

hic

hic

Would you rather have a head the size of a tennis ball

OR

feet the size of watermelons?

Would you rather only be able to communicate through emojis

OR

memes?

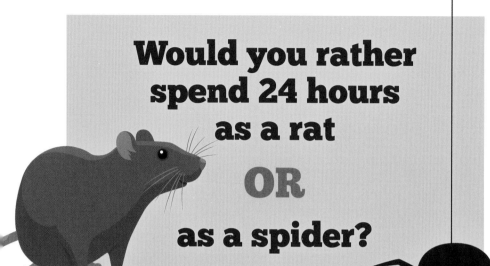

Would you rather spend 24 hours as a rat

OR

as a spider?

Would you rather have two eyes on the back of your head

OR

one eye by each ear?

Would you rather live in a place where it's always raining

OR

live in a place where it never rains at all?

Would you rather have to yell everything you speak

OR

only ever whisper?

Would you rather visit outer space

OR

any place on Earth?

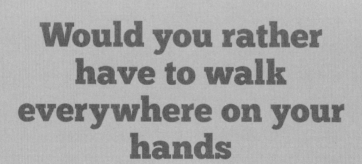

Would you rather have to walk everywhere on your hands

OR

pick up everything with your feet?

**Would you rather
meet someone famous
from history**

OR

**meet your favorite
character from TV?**

**Would you rather
live in a house made of
gingerbread cookies**

OR

**drive around in a car
made of jelly?**

Would you rather be covered in fur

OR

covered in scales?

Would you rather have the ability to time travel

OR

the ability to teleport?

**Would you rather
get a wedgie**

OR

**a wet willie every time
you tell a lie?**

**Would you rather be able
to go back in time to talk
to your past self**

OR

**travel into the
future to talk to your
future self?**

Would you rather have to drink everything out of a giant beach bucket

OR

out of a baby bottle?

Would you rather sleep four hours a day

OR

twenty hours a day for the rest of your life?

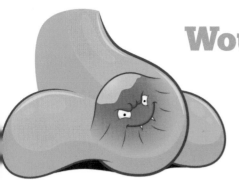

**Would you rather
have a huge
painful zit
on your nose**

OR

on your back?

**Would you rather
have hair you could
never cut**

OR

**hair that could
never grow past its
current length?**

Would you rather never know the time

OR

never know the day of the week?

Would you rather clean your teeth with someone else's old toothbrush

OR

chew someone else's pre-chewed gum?

Would you rather be allergic to your favorite food

OR

eat a rotten egg once a week?

Would you rather have to live without air conditioning

OR

never be able to use deodorant?

tasty

Cat Food

Would you rather eat a bowl of cat food

OR

a bowl of dog food?

Dog Food

Would you rather grow an extra set of ears

OR

a second nose?

Would you rather have a garden that grows candy

OR

your own personal arcade?

Would you rather win the lottery

OR

stumble upon an ancient treasure chest?

Would you rather tell terrible jokes for a huge crowd every week

OR

have to sit through an hour of terrible jokes every day?

Would you rather have transparent skin so everyone could see your veins and muscles

OR

be completely covered in hair and look like a walking pile of fur?

Would you rather your school have a drinking fountain filled with your favorite soda

OR

a french fry vending machine?

Would you rather be the lead actor in a terrible movie

OR

an extra in an award-winning film?

Would you rather be forced to sing along to every song you hear at the top of your lungs

OR

dance along to every song you hear in huge movements?

Would you rather get a paper cut every time you read a book

OR

bite your tongue every time you eat a meal?

58

Would you rather discover a long-hidden city

OR

a never-before-seen animal species?

Would you rather lose the ability to cry

OR

cry randomly for half an hour every day?

Would you rather get struck by lightning

OR

picked up by a tornado?

Would you rather pay five dollars every time you lie

OR

never lie again?

Would you rather always eat seriously burned food

OR

severely undercooked food?

Would you rather disturb a wasp's nest

OR

wake up a sleeping bear?

Would you rather bounce off every surface you touch

OR

never be able to jump again?

Would you rather walk through poison ivy

OR

swim through jellyfish-infested waters?

Would you rather sit on an ice-cold toilet seat

OR

a toilet seat that's warm from someone else's butt?

Would you rather have three legs

OR

three eyes?

Would you rather have to crawl everywhere on your hands and knees

OR

have to play "the floor is lava" wherever you go?

Would you rather step in dog poop

OR

have a bird poop on your shirt?

Would you rather spend an hour in the shark tank at the aquarium

OR

in the tiger exhibit at the zoo?

Would you rather have a mosquito bite between your toes

OR

in your belly button?

Would you rather wear all your clothes inside out

OR

all your clothes backwards for the rest of your life?

If you were in a movie, would you rather play a boring hero who wins at the end

OR

a fun villain who loses at the end?

Would you rather have a butt for a face

OR

a face for a butt?

Would you rather forget your all-time best memory

OR

be unable to forget your all-time worst memory?

**Would you rather have
a tail like a lizard**

OR

a tail like a raccoon?

**Would you rather have
ten-foot-long arms**

OR

ten-foot-long legs?

**Would you rather wear
nothing but neon colors**

OR

**nothing but black for
an entire year?**

Happy Birthday

Would you rather never eat birthday cake again

OR

never eat Halloween candy again?

Would you rather make beeping noises when you're stressed

OR

cry glitter?

Would you rather be able to breathe underwater

OR

have a private yacht at your disposal?

Would you rather write a bestselling novel

OR

direct an Oscar-winning movie?

Would you rather have terrible B.O. that you can't get rid of

OR

super-long nose hairs that you can't cut?

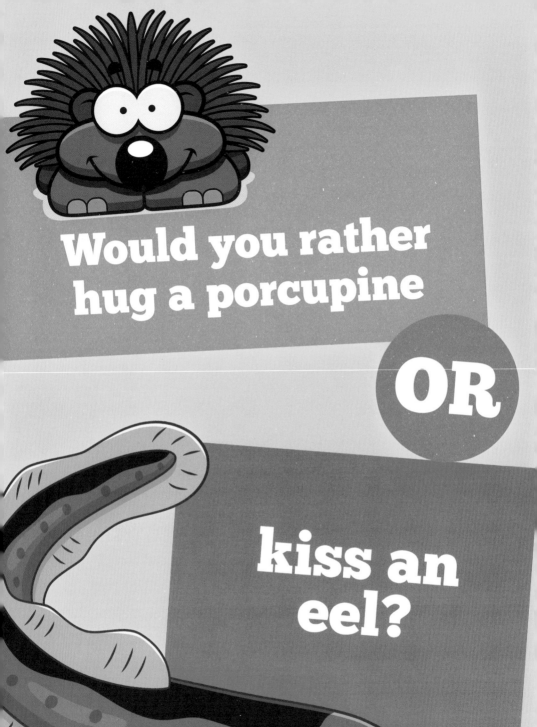

Would you rather shower every morning in freezing cold water

OR

in scalding hot water?

Would you rather only eat canned foods

OR

only eat food that grows from the ground?

Would you rather burp

OR

fart huge soap bubbles?

Would you rather brush your teeth with soap

OR

wash your hands with toothpaste?

Would you rather have five-day weekends and no summer vacation

OR

no weekends and a six-month vacation?

Weighing the Scales

Would you rather have a 1 in 10 chance of pooping whenever you fart

OR

a 1 in 10 chance of peeing whenever you sneeze?

Would you rather eat a live beetle

OR

be trapped in a room with a tarantula without knowing where it is?

**Would you rather
always feel like you
have to pee**

OR

**never know when
you're going to pee?**

**Would you rather
listen to the same song
for the rest of your life**

OR

**never be able to
listen to the same
song twice?**

Would you rather be a supporting character in the last book you read

OR

a supporting character in the last movie you watched?

Would you rather drink everything through your nose

OR

eat everything through your belly button?

Would you rather go back in time to meet your ancestors

OR

travel to the future to meet your great-great-grandchildren?

Would you rather be able to slow time by 25%

OR

be able to run 25% faster?

Would you rather be able to shapeshift

(but everyone can still tell it's you)

OR

be able to fly

(but only as fast as you can walk)?

Would you rather drink a glass of expired milk

OR

eat a grilled cheese sandwich made with moldy cheese?

Would you rather travel around in a kangaroo's pouch

OR

on a koala's back?

Would you rather accidentally call your friend "Mom"

OR

accidentally call your teacher "Mom"?

Would you rather
eat a live, wiggling fish

OR

a stinky day-old
fish that's starting
to go bad?

Would you rather
wear a smelly, sweaty
sock over your nose all
day at home

OR

wear your underwear as
a hat to school?

Would you rather have inch-long front teeth

OR

three-inch-long eyelashes?

Would you rather find a spider on your face

OR

inside your shirt?

Would you rather brush a crocodile's teeth

OR

give a lion a manicure?

Would you rather eat a small centipede that can bite you

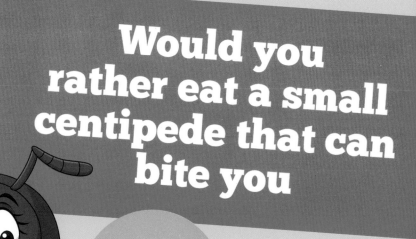

OR

a giant millipede that doesn't bite?

Would you rather have mushrooms growing all over your feet

OR

in your ears?

Would you rather be bitten by a bloodsucking leech

OR

stung by a giant wasp?

Would you rather be able to teleport only to places you've been before

OR

only to places you've never been?

Would you rather dance for five minutes in front of your whole class

OR

sing for five minutes in front of your whole class?

Would you rather be able to talk to pigeons

OR

transform into a pigeon at will?

Would you rather eat one of someone else's toenail clippings

OR

ten of someone else's hairs?

Would you rather be unable to close any door once it's opened

OR

be unable to open any door once it's closed?

Would you rather glow bright pink every time you're in front of your crush

OR

glow bright red whenever someone bothers you?

Would you rather wear ugly glasses that let you see perfectly

OR

very cool glasses that are always too blurry?

Would you rather receive a penny for every step you take

OR

receive fifteen dollars every time you run a mile?

Would you rather be an average person in the present day

OR

the ruler of a powerful country five hundred years ago?

Would you rather spend the rest of your life watching nothing but romantic comedies

OR

nothing but horror movies?

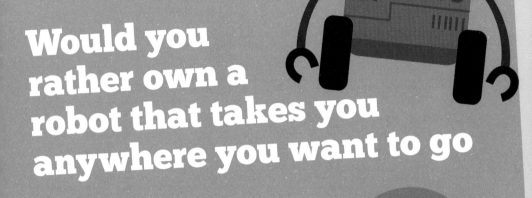

Would you rather own a robot that takes you anywhere you want to go

OR

a robot that will do any chores you don't want to do?

Would you rather have a pause button

OR

a rewind button for your life?

Would you rather have to pee in a litter box

OR

drink from a toilet?

Would you rather have snakes for hair

OR

icicles for hair?

91

Would you rather go vegan for a month

OR

only eat meat and dairy for a month?

Would you rather shower once every two weeks

OR

have to shower three times every day?

Would you rather have one wish granted today

OR

five wishes granted ten years from now?

Would you rather only eat raw vegetables for a year

OR

only eat TV dinners for a year?

Would you rather always have an annoying song stuck in your head

OR

rely on other people to scratch your itches?

Would you rather find a $100 bill floating in a dirty toilet

OR

a $10 bill in your pocket?

Would you rather master every musical instrument

OR

every type of sport?

Would you rather never have to work again

(You would have enough money.)

OR

never have to sleep again?

(You would suffer no negative effects.)

Would you rather stub your toe every morning

OR

get a paper cut every night?

Would you rather wake up in the middle of a desert

OR

wake up on a rowboat in the middle of the ocean?

Would you rather get trapped in a haunted house

OR

stuck in a city with zombies?

Would you rather be able to tell whenever someone is lying

OR

be able to get away with every lie you tell?

Would you rather be the worst football player in the NFL

OR

the best video game player?

Would you rather have to wear a bib whenever you eat

OR

use a sippy cup whenever you drink?

**Would you rather
sport a terrible hairstyle
for a month**

OR

**let your mom dress
you for a month?**

**Would you rather be
a gourmet chef but
have to prep and cook
all your meals**

OR

**be a terrible chef but be
able to order in?**

Would you rather punch a fish

OR

punch a bird?
(You have to catch it first.)

Would you rather be a fire-breathing dragon

OR

have a pet fire-breathing dragon?

Would you rather be a dog/cat with a human head

OR

a human with a dog/cat head?

Would you rather eat fried scorpions

OR

drink a worm smoothie?

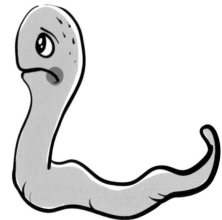

Would you rather
have to wear
sunglasses at night

OR

a headlamp on your
forehead all day?

Would you rather be
an actor on your
favorite TV show

OR

live for real inside the
world of that show?

Would you rather wear clown shoes full of Jell-O

OR

a ten-gallon hat full of stinky cheese?

Would you rather be tickled for an hour

OR

listen to an annoying laugh for 24 hours?

Would you rather have
a self-driving car

OR

live in a completely
automated home?

Would you rather begin
every sentence with
"hey loser"

OR

end every sentence with
"just kidding"?

Would you rather have
two long beaver teeth

OR

no teeth at all?

Would you rather meet an alien that landed on Planet Earth

OR

land on an alien planet yourself?

Would you rather spend 48 hours with both hands stuck in pickle jars

OR

with your head stuck in the stairwell?

Would you rather wear a cape

OR

an eye patch every day for a year?

(You can't tell anyone why.)

Would you rather be inside a porta-potty when it falls over

OR

smell like dog poop during your birthday party?

Would you rather drink a gallon of someone else's armpit sweat

OR

drink a gallon of your own toe sweat?

Would you rather have a giant tongue that you can't fit in your mouth

OR

a nose so big you can't see around it?

Would you rather have one exact clone of yourself

OR

five clones of yourself that are half your size?

**Would you rather have
to scream everything
you say**

OR

**have a voice so high
most people can't
hear you at all?**

**Would you rather
be invisible**

OR

**be visible but
look like a
terrifying lizard
monster?**

Impossible to Answer

Would you rather have to say everything that comes to mind

OR

only speak when someone asks you a direct question?

Would you rather burp

OR

fart at the end of every sentence?

Would you rather chew off your own toenails

OR

chew off someone else's fingernails?

Would you rather live all alone in a large cabin in the middle of the wilderness

OR

live in a big city but have no personal space?

**Would you rather
have superpowers that
you can't control**

OR

**be able to tell the
future but have no one
believe you?**

**Would you rather put
soap on your sandwich**

OR

**try to wash yourself with
ketchup and mustard?**

**Would you rather
pee your pants in
class once a week**

OR

**poop your pants in
private every day?**

**Would you rather
only be able to watch
one TV show for the
rest of your life**

OR

**only watch the first
episode of any TV show
for the rest of your life?**

Would you rather have to wear wet socks every day

OR

have to wear mittens 24/7?

Would you rather smell like poop and not know

OR

always smell poop that no one else notices?

Would you rather always feel like you have to sneeze but can't

OR

always have an itch on your back that you can't scratch?

Would you rather sweat mayonnaise

OR

poop candy?

Would you rather have to eat a handful of dirt before every meal

OR

stand upside down whenever you want to eat?

Would you rather eat a live snail with every meal

OR

eat a big bowl of live snails once a month?

Would you rather have a key that opens every door

OR

a pair of glasses that lets you read in any language?

Would you rather give up all drinks except water

OR

give up all food that's cooked in an oven?

Would you rather give up your phone for a year

OR

give up sugar for a year?

Would you rather have whatever you're thinking appear above your head for people to see

OR

have everything you do be filmed for an audience?

Would you rather 10% of the world have telepathy (the ability to read people's thoughts)

OR

10% of the world have telekinesis (the ability to move things with one's mind)?

(You would not belong to either group.)

Would you rather humans discover intelligent alien life

OR

discover a way to double the human lifespan?

Would you rather have to see a cockroach every day

OR

have spiders gain the ability to open doors?

Would you rather be able to control all land animals

OR

all creatures of the sea?

Would you rather have the face of a five-year-old and the body of a fifty-year-old

OR

the face of a fifty-year-old and the body of a five-year-old?

Would you rather sleep in a room with two tigers

OR

one hundred wasps?

Would you rather go all day with a huge booger hanging from your nose

OR

with B.O. that people can smell from a mile away?

Would you rather someone fart in your face

OR

have to carry around a rotten fish all day?

Would you rather poop in the bushes of your friend's house

OR

poop in your own bathroom sink?

Would you rather live in a house with ten thousand cockroaches

OR

ten thousand flies?

Would you rather
eat a clump of your own hair

OR

drink a cup of your own sweat?

Would you rather travel everywhere by pogo stick

OR

never be able to sit down?

**Would you rather
dress like a person from
five hundred years ago**

OR

have to talk like one?

**Would you rather
have the ability to see
ten minutes into
the future**

OR

**one hundred years
into the future?**

Would you rather wear the same underwear for a week

OR

the same socks for a month?

Would you rather have a photographic memory

OR

the world's highest IQ?

**Would you rather
be able to run fifty
miles an hour**

OR

**be able to fly at twenty
miles per hour?**

**Would you rather
only be able to speak
five hundred words a day**

OR

**never be able to say
words with the
letter "s"?**

Would you rather speak out of your butt

OR

be the only person in the world who doesn't speak out of their butt?

Would you rather live in a stable filled with barn animals

OR

have a bunch of barn animals live in your house?

Would you rather have to clean a huge mess in your kitchen every day

OR

cook every single meal you eat?

Would you rather give your enemy unlimited access to all the pictures on your phone

OR

all of your text messages?

Would you rather swim with piranhas

OR

sleep in a boat being followed by a killer whale?

Would you rather eat a whole raw onion

OR

a bulb of raw garlic?

Would you rather not cut your fingernails

OR

toenails for a year?

Would you rather announce every time you're about to fart

OR

have the world's loudest possible fart?

Would you rather a museum displayed your most embarrassing photos

OR

a novel recounted your most embarrassing experience?

Would you rather tell a lie for a good reason

OR

tell the truth for a bad one?

**Would you rather
eat every meal with
someone who chews
louder than a truck**

OR

**with someone who spits
across the room when
they eat?**

**Would you rather
be unknown in your
life and famous after
your death**

OR

**famous during your
life but unknown after
your death?**

Would you rather take a pill a day for all your needed nutrients but never eat anything again

OR

eat whatever you want but never truly feel full?

Would you rather be unable to keep anyone else's secrets

Psst!

OR

have someone else tell all of your secrets?

Would you rather be
so afraid of heights that
you can't go above the
second floor of a building

OR

be so afraid of the sun
that you can only leave
the house at night?

Would you rather only
be able to wash your
hair twice a year

OR

only be able to
check your phone once
a week?

Would you rather be punished for a crime you didn't commit

OR

never receive credit for your greatest accomplishments?

Would you rather spend the rest of your life with popcorn stuck in your teeth

OR

with an eyelash stuck in your eye?

Would you rather have the ability to remember every fact you ever learn

OR

know everything about a person before you meet them?

Would you rather have complete control over your emotions

OR

be able to control the emotions of other people?

Would you rather use vinegar for eyedrops

OR

sandpaper for toilet paper?

Would you rather puke slugs

OR

poop bricks?

(You would puke and poop the same amount that you do now.)

**Would you rather
eat jelly from between
someone's toes**

OR

**canned cheese from
someone's armpit?**

**Would you rather
fight a hyperintelligent
monkey**

OR

**a horse that knows
karate?**

Would you rather be the only person in the whole world who has magic powers

OR

live in a world where everyone else has magic powers?

Would you rather be able to take back anything you say

OR

hear any conversation that is about you?

Would you rather always be hungry no matter how much you eat

OR

always be tired no matter how much you sleep?

Would you rather eat an entire bag of dead, rotting flies

OR

have live flies come out of your nose every time you sneeze for the next ten years?

Would you rather live
next to an active volcano

OR

in an extreme flood
zone?

Would you rather use
fish-scented toothpaste

OR

ham-scented deodorant?

Would you rather eat
mayo with a spoon

OR

drink ketchup through
a straw?

Would you rather eat
cheese pizza with
dessert toppings

OR

ice cream mixed with
pizza toppings?

Would you rather
be immortal on a
mortal planet

OR

be mortal on an
immortal planet?

144